The Boston Tea Party

History Detective 1

The English Reading Tree

Published by G-L-R (Great Little Read)

Written by Keith Goodman

Reading age for this book: 7+

Reading age for the series will vary but starts at seven

The English Reading Tree Series has been written for children aged seven and over. It is the perfect tool for parents to get their children into the habit of reading.

This book has been created to entertain and educate young minds and is packed with information and trivia and lots of authentic images that bring the topic alive.

TABLE OF CONTENTS

Meet Ben

Hi, I'm Benjamin, but you can call me Ben. I'm the History

Detective

Don't ask how, but just by closing my eyes and thinking of a date

for a couple of minutes, I can physically get back there. The only

trouble is, I can't stay very long, and the people in the past can't see me. I become one of them, and the thing is, I never know who that will be. Whatever happens in the past, I see it through the eyes of somebody that was somehow involved in the event I'm investigating. Sounds complicated? Not really, just sit back, and I will take you with me on my journey of historical discovery.

It's kinda exciting being able to do this, but please don't tell anyone; let's keep it between you and me.

One thing I have learned is that our ancestors are not much different from us, and some of them can be really cool, while others are complete idiots.

I'm not a freak, and I reckon I get this power from my grandmother. She claimed she could time travel, but nobody believed her, not even me. True, one time, she thought that she had the power to fly, but she was a lovely lady.

She once told me that she had gone back to prehistoric times and that dinosaurs were lovely creatures.

She said that she had even had a baby T-Rex as a pet, but that's another story.

Today, I'm thinking about the lead up to the American War of Independence and particularly, the Boston Tea Party.

I know nothing about this event, and I have a test tomorrow in school about it.

Was it a tea party? If so, who was invited, and how come nobody got to drink any tea?

I'm closing my eyes…

My head is spinning, and there is a strange smell in the air that is definitely not tea or coffee.

When I get a whiff of an unusual odor, I know that it's working. Did you know that since I started going back in history, one of the things that I have come to expect is that the past doesn't smell like today?

Not being funny, but our ancestors were more than a bit dirty. Nice, but dirty. Well, okay, sometimes not even nice, but still dirty.

So, here I am in Boston (hopefully), and the date is Thursday, December 16, 1773.

And the time is 8:30 AM.

The countdown is eleven hours to the party! I hear that it's going to be fancy dress.

Breakfast at Will's Tavern

Green Dragon Tavern, Union Street.

I half-opened my eyes, but before I did, I had already smelt the aroma of ham and eggs that was in the air. I was sitting on my own near the window of what seemed to be a tavern.

Wow, this place isn't like a KFC or McDonald's, it is dark, and the tables are all old and stained. There is sawdust scattered over the floor, and the people that are passing by the window are all dressed strangely. Some of them are wearing white wigs. A young lad runs past the window pushing a large round hoop with a stick. I guess this is the colonial version of the PS4. I'm dressed in breeches, brown boots, itchy woolen shirt, and a waistcoat. At least I fit in with everybody else. I wonder what my name is. I am about to find out.

"Wake up George, how can you fall asleep at breakfast?"

The man who had just spoken was standing at the side of the counter with a cloth in his hands. He was cleaning cups. He was fairly young looking with long black hair and piercing green eyes. He was wearing a white apron with black breeches.

"Sorry, I must have nodded off," I replied, "I had a late-night."

It looked like I was the only customer. The man came over to my table, carrying a wooden tray with two small, white cups on it. "I know what you need, George. Try this." He handed me a cup of tea, and I took a sip. It was sweet and milky, but had an amazing flavor.

"Now, this is what you call a cup of tea, George. Not like the rubbish, the English are sending over."

"Nice," I agreed.

He winked. "It's Dutch. That's why we are drinking it the Dutch way."

"How do you mean?"

"With milk. Most customers like it black and sweet, but I knew that you would savor how good it is with milk."

The door opened, and a man in a bowler hat and hunting jacket put his head around it. "The meeting is on later today. Are you coming, Will?"

"Will nodded and raised his cup of tea. I'll be there, Jim, I wouldn't miss this for the world. There's a plan afoot, lad, and after last night's drinking session in the Dragon, I think we are finally going to teach those British idiots a lesson that they will never forget. I've got a sore head. We all drank too much rum."

At least I knew his name, but very little else. I had heard about the Boston Tea Party, and I knew the date, but still didn't have a clue about what it was about. That's why I was here to find out. Maybe Will could clue me in. He looked like he was the talkative type.

"Big day, then today, Will?" I inquired.

He looked around the room furtively, as if he expected soldiers to jump out and arrest him. He ignored my question. "Do you like the tea?"

"Yeah, it terrific." Actually, I prefer coffee or chocolate milk, but I wasn't going to get into anything controversial.

"Plenty more crates of this if you want some. My acquaintances brought it in last night. Shall I put your name down for some?" He reached into his pocket and brought out a notebook. "How many tins, George?"

"Err, ten." That was the first number that came into my head.

He raised his eyebrows, licked his lips, and then licked his pencil. "You must drink a lot of tea in your household, George. I think I can manage it but," he winked, "You will have to wait until tomorrow."

"Why, how big are the tins?"

"You've got such a sense of humor, George. They are the same size as the last lot you bought."

"Oh yeah, it slipped my memory." By the time Will gets round to bringing them, I will be long gone. I'll play him along.

He took a watch on a silver chain from out of his waistcoat."We had better be going if we want to get a good seat in the Green Dragon. I reckon that it's going to be packed. There's a lot of money to be made tonight; I'll tell you the plan when we meet Jonas and his Indian friend."

"Aye, I was wondering about the plan, Will." Whatever plan Will had, it looked like it involved tea and a meeting in somewhere called the Green Dragon? My guess is that it is a bar or a tavern, but why are we going there, and how come Will expects to be making money? There was only one way to find out. I watched Will put his coat on, put a closed sign up in the window, and followed him out into the street. Outside smelt of horse manure and lard. I tagged along at his side, savoring the atmosphere.

Boston was not what I expected it to be. There were not that many people on the streets, and only the occasional horse or horse-drawn carriage went past. Despite the lack of people, some of the buildings were very impressive. This included the one where we stopped. The Green Dragon was dark and cramped inside but was bustling with people, many of whom acknowledged both myself and Will. It looked like whoever I was; I was very popular amongst the locals. Will didn't seem interested in talking to anybody, and he led me to some stairs in the corner, and we descended into an even more cramped cellar.

Fact Check: Boston 1773

The Boston Massacre didn't help to calm the conflict between the

British and Americans

Boston had a population of around 15,000 in 1773 and was

known as a hotbed for political protest against the British.

Bostonians were a tough breed and felt that they were getting a bad

deal off the British. After all, Britain was thousands of miles away.

Why should the British Parliament decide how Americans should

live their lives?

Why were the British so unaware of the revolutionary wind that was sweeping through its American Colonies? Don't forget that there was no internet in the 1800s, so news traveled slowly and was not very reliable. It depended on the person carrying it.

Protest for Americans living in the 1800s was based on a principle of what was right and what was wrong, but for the British, taxation of the colonies was solely about money.

The British Government had sent troops to America to fight in the French and Indian War. It finished in victory for the Americans and the British, but it had been an extremely costly war for Britain.

The British King, George III, wanted to get some of the money back, so he decided to tax the American Colonies as a way of doing this. It was also seen by the British as a way of keeping control over the rebellious Americans.

Britain was in debt and blamed the French and Indian War. They wanted America to pay back some of the cost, and in 1765 the British Parliament passed the **Stamp Act**. This act meant than virtually any piece of paper that had writing on it needed to have a stamp. This included legal documents, newspapers, and even playing cards.

In 1767, the **Townshend Acts** taxed items such as tea, lead, glass, paint, and paper.

The British thought that the taxes were justified, but the Americans disagreed and began to protest. They even stopped buying British products. Americans said, 'No taxation without representation in the British Parliament.'

In March 1770, American protestors jeered at British troops in Boston and began to throw stones and snowballs at them. The British troops panicked and opened fire. Five colonists were killed, and another six were wounded. This became known as the **Boston Massacre**. It served to make the tension between the Americans and British close to breaking point.

In the end, the British got rid of the taxes on everything except the tea. Even with the tea tax, the sale of British tea was cheaper than tea that was being smuggled into the colonies.

For the Americans, it was not about the money. The protest was based on the principle of being controlled by a country that was thousands of miles away. If the British could tax tea, then in the future, they could impose taxation on anything.

In Boston, by December 1773, the colonists had become very angry.

The Green Dragon

I have become a colonial man for the day, and what a day it

turned out to be

"We are not going to take it any more off the British," said the

man in the three-corner hat, long grey coat and breeches."

"No more," shouted the thirty or so men gathered in the room

deep below the Green Dragon. Will and I had settled on to a narrow

bench in the corner, with two other of his friends. One was a blonde-haired youth with crossed-eyes, and the other a Native American wearing a powdered wig, vivid green waistcoat, and white riding breeches.

I looked around the room. It was full of men—angry men who waved their fists about in the air and shouted about how bad the British were.

The man standing on a chest motioned for them to be silent, but it took a while before they became quiet, enough for him to speak again. When he did, his voice was solemn.

"Do we agree that enough is enough?"

There were murmurs from the room, and I found myself joining in and shouting, "Yes, down with the British."

The man on the chest waited for the noise to fade away.

"Then, the plan is for tonight. I have already spoken to the people who will join me. Gentlemen, what we do tonight will be remembered by Americans down the centuries. The story of our attack on those British ships in the harbor and their cargo of tea will take on the stuff of legends. After tonight, the British King and all of his advisers will understand once and for all that they cannot mess with Americans. They cannot keep the Sons of Liberty down."

A rousing cheer went up in the room, and the man stepped off the chest and began mingling with the crowd. There was much backslapping, handshaking, and laughter.

"Wrong on at least two counts there," said the Native American.

"George, sorry, but you've not met Ahmik have you," said Will

"Pleased to meet you, George," said Ahmik. His smile showed off brilliant white teeth, which he was obviously very proud of. "Most white folks call me Horse as the Mohawk language is beyond them."

The blonde-haired boy cut in. "I'm Jonas, but everybody calls me Brains."

"That's because he ain't got any," laughed Horse.

"What do you mean, wrong on two counts?" I asked Horse.

"Well, George. These lads that call themselves the Sons of Liberty are angry enough, but they are all a bit like our friend Brains here. They are not that clever. For a start, those three ships that they are going to board tonight are not British; they are American. And for seconds, if they think that the British are going to let them destroy all that tea and do nothing, they are stupid."

"Don't listen to Horse," said Will. "It's just his opinion."

Horse shook his head, but the smile still hadn't left his face. His teeth were dazzling me. "You mark my words, George; I'm what's called an intellectual. After what those idiots are going to do tonight, it's war. Do you think that this lot are going to be able to beat the British?"

"Err, no. That would seem to be impossible," I replied.

"Enough of this, gentlemen," said Will. Those Sons of Liberty might be trying to get their freedom from British tax oppression, but what we are going to get is something far more valuable. Money!"

"And the beauty of your plan, Will," joked Horse. "Is that nobody is going to miss the tea that we steal."

"Yes, it's a perfect plan, even though I say it myself."

You're a genius, Will," said Brains.

Steal? Now that was a new one. "Shall we go through the plan again?" I asked. They stopped talking and looked at me.

"Your job is easy," said Will. All you need to do is follow me onto the ship, and start throwing the crates over the side."

"My lads will be underneath with Brains, ready to pick up the crates before they get ruined with seawater."

"Don't forget the disguises," whispered Horse conspiratorially. "I've already tried mine on."

Now, I was confused. "Disguises?"

Will slapped me heartily on the back. "Don't worry about that, George; I've got disguises for both of us. Everybody is dressing up."

Brains raised his tankard of beer is a salute. "It's going to be a party atmosphere tonight. Those British don't know what's coming."

"Yeah," I said almost to myself. "I guess none of you know what's coming."

"What was that?" Asked Will

I changed the subject. "I said, I'm looking forward to what's

coming."

They all raised their tankards and said in unison. "Let's drink a

toast to what's coming."

This time I kept my mouth shut.

Fact Check: The Three Ships

A common idea about the Boston Tea Party is that the protesters boarded three British ships that were in the harbor. The colonials were angry with King George and wanted to dump his tea into the harbor. What actually happened is different.

That night in December 1773, the protesters boarded the Eleanor, the Dartmouth, and the Beaver. All of these ships were built in America and owned by Americans. Two of the ships were not even cargo vessels; they were whalers.

At this period in history, whale oil was a very important commodity. Two of the ships had just delivered whale oil to the port of London. To ensure that they didn't go back to America with an empty hold, they were loaded with crates of tea and other stuff.

To get an idea of the atmosphere of America in 1773, you need to understand that not all Americans hated the British. Some (mainly wealthy) considered themselves more British than American. It was probable that the owners of the ships were British sympathizers.

The tea that was thrown into Boston Harbour did not belong to the King. It was owned by a private firm called the East India Company. For the company, the loss of 340 crates of tea must have been devastating. In today's money, the tea would have been worth around two million dollars. Now that's a lot of cups of tea.

For those people reading, who are tea enthusiasts, the tea that was destroyed was from China, and it was green tea. The more traditional Indian tea didn't come from India until plantations were set up in the country in the 1830s.

Preparing to Board the Dartmouth

I went back down Union Street to Will's Tavern, which was conveniently called Will's Tavern, so it was easy to remember. Here, he cooked me a fine lunch of mutton stew and salt beans with watered-down beer. While we were drinking our tea, he told me the plan, and I realized that he wasn't a patriot or a Son of Liberty at all. Will was a tea smuggler who had just thought up the best way to get rich without anybody being the wiser.

The British would blame the Americans for destroying their tea out of anger against the Tea Act, and the Americans would blame the English for trying to control them without giving them a voice in the British Parliament.

Will and his gang, which included me, would slip through the middle unseen and make off with loads of tea. The only thing that I believe concerned him about the evening work ahead was that the tea on the ships was from China and was green. He said he didn't like it very much though it was popular with the colonists.

Brains arrived late afternoon with a wry smile on his face. He was wearing a full-length hunting frock and looked slightly different. I didn't get it at first but then realized that he had darkened his hair and face.

Will looked at him with horror at what he was seeing. When Brains took off his coat, the horror turned to anger, though I found it hard not to laugh. I pretended I was having a coughing fit.

Will came from behind the bar, "What have you done to yourself, Brains?"

Brains looked shocked at the reaction he had caused. " You said to dress-up as an Indian."

"Yeah?"

"I couldn't get the exact thing that they wear. It's called a Kurta, but a Kurta is just a long shirt."

"How did somebody like you know that?"

"You forgot about the Gupta family that live two doors down from me."

"The road sweeper?"

"Yeah, him."

"And your face and hair?"

"Soot and charcoal. Does it make me look like an Indian?"

"Yeah, from India, but unfortunately, not like a Mohawk Indian," said Will.

That took the smile off the face of Brains, but before he had time to react, the door of the tavern opened and in walked a huge brown bear.

We all froze, and the bear roared, then laughed. "It's me, Will."

The events of the last two minutes seemed to have fazed Will. He didn't look a happy man. "Horse?" He inquired.

The bear pulled its own head off and shouted, "I had you all worried for a second, admit it."

Will shook his head in disbelief. "Horse, why have you come dressed as a bear?"

"You said, fancy dress, Will. Dressing up like a Mohawk is not fancy dress for me. If you haven't noticed, boys, I am a Mohawk."

It was my turn to say something. "Don't you think that seeing us walking down the street with a big brown bear will look a bit conspicuous?"

"No more than walking down the street with a sub-continental India who has obviously used charcoal to darken his hair and face," replied Horse.

"You don't think that it looks convincing enough?" asked Brains

"Enough," shouted Will. "Let's just go and get the tea, shall we? I have to say, Horse, I am possibly more comfortable walking to the harbor in the company and an Indian, rather than a bear."

Horse looked hurt. "Will, you don't understand symbolism."

Will shrugged, handed me a couple of Mohawk feathers, and made his way towards the door. "What's symbolic about being a brown bear?"

"It's not about fitting in with everybody. It's my way of expressing to the world that we are Americans and not British. What's more American than a brown bear?"

Will opened the door and strode out into the street. "How about a Mohawk Indian. And, George, put your feathers in.

The Tension Mounts

On the 28th of November 1773, the first of the three tea ships to

arrive in Boston from England was the Dartmouth. The ship's

captain was James Hall. As was standard at the time, the Dartmouth

went directly to Rowe's Warf, but because there was already ill-

feeling against the ships' arrival, the merchant John Rowe did not

want to see violence on his property. The ship was moved to

Griffin's Warf.

Boston Harbour was watched over by the British, who had around a hundred cannons at the mouth of the harbor in Castle William. The Colonists wanted the ship to sail back to London, but it was the law of the time that when a ship entered the harbor, it could not sail out with the same cargo still on board. The ship could not leave Boston without the Governor's permission, which was not granted. Ships had twenty days to unload their cargo. The Americans didn't want the cargo. The deadline would expire on December 17.

The owner of the Dartmouth was given until three in the afternoon of December 16, to obtain the permit necessary for the ship to leave Boston. He rode fifteen miles to meet the governor, but as expected, permission was withheld.

The Dartmouth had to stay in Boston Harbour or risk running the British cannons to escape. Not a great choice.

The fuse had been lit, and the Boston Tea Party was about to begin.

Most of the people that lived in Boston went down to Griffin's Warf that night to see the fun. The 'Indians' went on board the ships and destroyed 342 chests of tea. People watched in almost complete silence from the Warf.

This was low tide, so there was barely three feet of water under the ships. The estimated forty-two tons of tea formed mini-mountains at the sides of the ships. People climbed onto these piles to push them over so that the tea would be ruined.

Even though the protesters were armed with hatchets, they were civilized. The captain of the Beaver was concerned about his other cargo, which was fine English furniture. He was told that as long as he stayed out of the way, only the tea would be damaged. The patriots were true to their words and very carefully took the tea but left all of the other cargo, which included French Brandy. They even replaced a broken padlock.

The patriots worked as quickly as they could because they were afraid that the British Royal Navy would attack them, but this never happened.

When they had finished their work, the Patriots walked away to the music of the fife (flute)

The party was over, and everybody returned to their homes.

The path to the revolution had started, though on this night nobody believed it, especially the British.

A Strange Party

Boston was buzzing with people all going the same way. They were heading to Griffin's Warf. Horse went on ahead, and Will explained the plan.

It was early evening, and I could feel the chill in the air. My disguise, like Will's, was pathetic. We had a couple of feathers stuck in our hair. Now that's going to fool people (not). Will had a hatchet stuck in his belt, and as we passed other small groups of 'Mohawks,' I noticed that everyone else was also carrying axes or hatchets. Everyone except me, but I didn't mind, those things looked sharp, and I just knew that I would cut myself if I had one.

Will reached into his pocket and produced a small box. "Here, George, put some of this on."

"What's that," I joked. "Makeup?"

"No, its coal dust, but it will do the trick and darken your face a bit."

"I thought we were going as Indians; if I put this on my face, I will look like a coal miner."

"Coal miner, Indians, what does it matter? Just put it on and shut up."

I did what I was told. It seemed like the whole of Boston was out on the streets, and they were all in high spirits.

We arrived at the Warf, and here things were getting organized. We fell in line with a group of men disguised as Mohawks and marched to the music of a flute towards the ships. The crowd let out a cheer, as we got closer. I felt like a superstar. Smashing up the tea chests had just become a spectator sport. If only these laughing

Bostonians that surrounded me knew what tonight's work was going to start, I wondered if they would be so happy and tranquil?

I noticed that there were a couple of people who were in charge and directing the boarding of the ships. They barked out their orders, and everybody did what they were told, but not us.

"We need to get close to the Dartmouth," whispered Will.

"Why?"

"Because Horse and some men will be waiting underneath her with a raft. We throw the crates down, and they will load them up and take them away."

"What if somebody sees us?" I asked.

"We tell them that we are taking the chests further out into the harbor, where the water is deeper."

The men were dividing up into three groups, and Will held back and joined the group going on board the Dartmouth.

It seemed like an age that we waited to go onboard. It reminded me of queuing up at an airport and waiting to get on board a plane. "What's happening?" I hissed in Will's ear.

"They are probably negotiating with the captain to let us aboard peaceably."

"And if he refuses?"

Will shrugged, and just at that moment, the leader of our group appeared at the ship's rail. He held up his ax and some candles.

"Gentlemen, board the vessel but damage nothing except the tea. For those of you going into the hold, take these candles but light them carefully as I am told there is dynamite as well as tea in there."

Brains appeared as if by magic and winked at Will.

Will nodded with his head for us to move towards the ship. "You are going to see why Brains is so important to the plan. He is not the brightest spark but is the strongest man I have ever met, and those chest weight around one hundred and fifty pounds."

"Won't they smash when we throw them over the side?"

"No, the water will lessen the impact. Even if they leak a little bit, we just have to load them up onto the raft and take them to my warehouse."

The men scrambled on board the Dartmouth and opened the hatches to the hold where the cargo was stored.

The first of the chests were passed up, and the men descended on them like wild animals, tore the tops off, and started to empty the tea over the side.

We got to the first chest and carried it to the back of the ship.

Everybody was so concentrated on their work that we were not challenged.

Will was right about the chests; they were heavy.

We threw the first over the side and heard a satisfying splash.

When I looked over and down into the dark depths of the water, I could see Horse and several other men loading the chest onto a large raft. They worked quickly in semi-darkness. Horse had taken off his bear suit.

This looked like it was a well-coordinated operation and one that the history books missed.

"How many of these crates are on board?" I asked Will.

"I'm not sure," he replied, but about a hundred and fifty, I think."

It was going to be a long and gruelling night's work.

In the end, we managed to get sixteen crates over the side, and it took us three hours. The raft could only hold one crate at a time, so we had to wait for it to be unloaded and brought back. One of the crates broke on impact with the water, but it was still carried away with the tea spilling out into the saltwater.

As we worked, the crates seemed to be getting lighter. Maybe we were getting used to the weight.

The answer was much simpler than this, but I would only find it out later.

As the night dragged on, people on board began to get edgy, and there was talk about the British Royal Navy or British Troops arriving to arrest us. In the end, nobody came, and we were allowed to finish our work.

When everybody started to leave, we hung back and made our way down the Warf to Will's warehouse.

Inside the warehouse, it was party time. Horse and the men who had helped bring the tea were smoking their pipes and drinking beer. They cheered when Will went through the door. We had done it. We had robbed tea from the Boston Tea Party, and nobody was going to be any the wiser. Brains lit up a long clay pipe and poured himself a tankard of beer.

"I think I will have a cup of tea," said Will, using his hatchet to take the top off one of the chests.

"That's strange looking tea, Will," said Horse. He put his hand inside the chest, pulled out a handful of black powder. He smelt it. "This is gunpowder."

"Gunpowder," shouted everybody in unison.

They all rushed to the boxes and began pulling the lids off.

They were all gunpowder except four. That must have been the first few that we had thrown overboard.

Will looked like a man who had just won the lottery and realized that he had lost the ticket.

The party atmosphere had been extinguished.

"We've made a big mistake," Said Will

"It's a disaster," shouted Horse.

"Let's go back to the harbor and go fishing for tea," said Brains.

"Should you be smoking that pipe so close to the gunpowder? I asked

Facts and Trivia

The firm that was damaged by the Boston Tea Party was the East India Company. This company brought in spices and cotton from India, but most of the tea came from China. In fact, tea plantations were not set up in India until the mid-1830s.

Almost a quarter of the tea that was ruined in the Boston Tea Party was green tea. We know from historical records that both George Washington and Thomas Jefferson enjoyed a cup of green tea and loved a particular type that was called Hyson.

No, the Boston Tea Party did not start the War of Independence, and a lot of people, including George Washington, denounced acts of violent behavior and lawlessness.

Rather than the act itself, it was the reaction of the British Government that pushed the American Colonies towards war. Rather than understanding the grievances, all that the British King and his government wanted to do was punish the colonists and show them who was in charge.

Some of the sanctions imposed by the British made Americans very angry. Boston Harbour was closed, and many elected American leaders were replaced with others loyal to the British Crown.

Even though a lot of Americans disassociated themselves from the Boston Tea Party itself, they became angry with the total lack of justice in the colonies and the fact that America had no voice in the British Parliament.

Rather than trying to disguise themselves by dressing up as Mohawks, the rebels that boarded the ships were using dressing up as a symbolic gesture to show that they were free spirits and American, not British.

The actual term, Boston Tea Party, was not used at the time of the incident. The first time that it was recorded in print was in 1825. The word 'party' was used to describe a party (group) of men and not a celebration like a birthday party. In 1773, it was referred to as the act of destroying tea in Boston Harbour, which was not really a clickbait headline.

The Boston Tea Party is famous, but did you know that there were other 'tea parties' in the colonies. In the Philadelphia Tea Party, no tea was destroyed, but the captain of a ship carrying tea was threatened and told to take all of it back to England, which he did.

In Charleston, seven chests of tea were thrown into the harbor. The interesting thing about this 'tea party' was the date. It took place on December 3, 1773. This was thirteen days before the Boston Tea Party.

In March 1774, there was the Boston Tea Party, part two (The sequel). Like most sequels, it wasn't as impressive as the original. About sixty men boarded a ship called the Fortune and dumped thirty chests of tea into the harbor.

The amount of tea that was dumped into the water during the Boston Tea Party was enough to fill 18.5 million teabags. Now that's a lot of tea.

Apparently, the only man injured during the rebellious act was John Crane. He was hit by a falling tea crate and thought to be dead. He was hidden under a pile of wood shavings in a carpenter's shop that was near the harbor. Miraculously, he woke up with just a very bad headache.

Back Home

So, I seem to have suffered no injuries on my trip back to 1773, which is just as well considering there's school tomorrow.

What have I learned about the Boston Tea Party?

I've learned that any event that starts off with a noble motive can be hijacked by people who are only taking part for their own self-interest.

It is clear that the British were not acting very reasonably with Colonial Americans, and who knows, if they had permitted American representation in the British Houses of Parliament in London, American History could have been very different.

Will, Horse, and Brains tried to use the Boston Tea Party to make money, but it didn't work out.

You will not find any record of an explosion that night. I have just done a Google search. Little people like Will, Horse, and Brains get forgotten over the centuries because they are not major players in major events. Remember, in all of the great events of our time; it is the ordinary people that play the biggest part and do all of the hard work.

Anyway, that's enough from me. I wonder what my next trip into the past will be.

Check it out, and we can go there together.

Thank you for Reading this Book

You can visit the English Reading Tree Page by clicking:

Visit Amazon's Keith Goodman Page (Mailing List)

Books in the English Reading Tree Series by Keith Goodman include:

1 The Titanic for Kids

2 Shark Facts for Kids

3 Solar System Facts for Kids

4 Dinosaur Facts for Kids

5 American Facts and Trivia for Kids

6 Christmas Facts and Trivia for Kids

7 Space Race Facts for Kids

8 My Titanic Adventure for Kids

9 Save the Titanic for Kids

10 Halloween Facts and Trivia for Kids

67 The Titanic Diary for Kids

68 Myths and Legends for Kids

69 The Loch Ness Monster for Kids

Other books by the same author:

Meet the Boneheads

The School Bully: Meet the Boneheads

Books From the For School Series

1 Native American History for School Grades 3 – 5

2 Colonial American History for School Grades 3 – 5

3 The American Revolution for School Grades 3 – 5

4 The American Industrial Revolution for School Grades 3 – 5

5 The American Civil War for School Grades 3 – 5

Attributions

File:Green Dragon Tavern1.jpg

BPL / CC BY (https://creativecommons.org/licenses/by/2.0)

The author and license can be found here

https://commons.wikimedia.org/wiki/File:Green_Dragon_Tavern1.jpg

Made in the USA
Middletown, DE
30 July 2022